GE

LAND

of the Kimberley

GW00862468

by Ian Tyler

DEPARTMENT OF CONSERVATION AND LAND MANAGEMENT

Rocks exposed in the Kimberley record a geological story that takes in the last 1900 million years of the Earth's history.

The oldest rocks form the Lennard Hills in the western Kimberley and the Bow River Hills and the Halls Creek ridges in the eastern Kimberley. They were formed between 1920 and 1790 million years ago and represent a period during which an ancient ocean was gradually being closed. At this time, the Kimberley was part of a larger continent to the north, but was drifting towards a continent which made up the rest of northern Australia. A mountain range probably formed along the southern and eastern margins of the Kimberley "continent", between 1865 and 1850 million years ago, similar to the Andes along the Pacific coast of South America today.

The Kimberley finally collided with the rest of northern Australia about 1830 million years ago. These events produced major upheavals in the Earth's crust, during which huge volumes of molten rock (magma) were produced. This reached the Earth's surface as lava erupted by volcanoes, or remained within the crust and solidified to form intrusions of granite and gabbro. The tremendous forces at work during this time buckled rocks into folds, or broke them along faults, burying some rocks deep in the crust where they were metamorphosed, or changed, by the action of pressure and heat. This caused new minerals such as garnet and mica to grow within the rocks. In the most extreme conditions, the rocks began to melt.

The collision uplifted the older rocks and sediment was eroded from them and deposited in the Kimberley Basin, which underlies much of the Kimberley Plateau (forming the central part of the Kimberley region), until about 1800 million years ago. At that time, sediment deposited by a major river system flowing from the north covered the whole region.

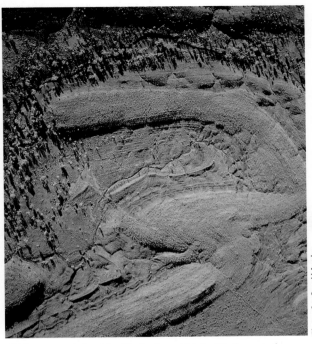

Photo - Ian Oswald-Jacobs

Folding caused when the Kimberley collided with the rest of northern Australia

Since 1790 million years ago, the Kimberley region has periodically become geologically active, usually in response to events occurring at the margins of the continent. Between 1600 and 1500 million years ago, sedimentary rocks were deposited in the Birrindudu Basin, which now underlies the Tanami Desert. Fossil stromatolites are found in magnesium-rich limestones (dolomites) of this age in the Osmond Range, north of the Bungle Bungle Range. More sedimentary rocks were deposited in the eastern Kimberley about 1200 million years ago and soon after were intruded by the Argyle diamond pipe.

About 1000 million years ago, earth movements folded, faulted and metamorphosed the rocks, and large folds developed in rocks exposed on the Yampi Peninsula. Between 700 and 600 million years ago, much of the Earth was caught in the grip of an ice age. Glacial deposits from this time can be seen throughout southern, central and northern Australia, and are well preserved in the Kimberley.

About 550 million years ago, the Halls Creek Fault system, which can be traced from the edge of the Great Sandy Desert all the way to Darwin, formed. This is a system of wrench faults on which movement is horizontal, similar to the San Andreas Fault in California. The rocks on the western side of the fault have moved to the left (south-west) relative to those on the eastern side. The margin of the Kimberley Basin crumpled during this south-westward movement, resulting in spectacular folding in the King Leopold Range.

A period of volcanic activity followed, with the outpouring of extensive flows of basalt in the eastern Kimberley. Overlying rocks in the Ord and Bonaparte basins were deposited in a shallow sea about 540 million years ago, at a time when the variety of life within the oceans underwent an explosion, with many different forms of plant and animal life being preserved as fossils.

Sedimentary rocks began to be deposited in the Canning Basin (which today is roughly synonymous with the floodplain of the Fitzroy River) from about 500 million years ago. About 375 million years ago, in Devonian times, the sea deepened and a remarkable system of barrier reefs began to form. The reefs fringed three sides of a land mass, formed by the Kimberley Plateau, extending into the Bonaparte Basin. On the fourth side, the Halls

Creek Fault system again became active, and sediment that was eroded from active fault scarps accumulated as sandstones and conglomerate deposits. These now form the Ragged Ranges, the Bungle Bungle Range and Kununurra's Hidden Valley.

Between 310 and 270 million years ago an ice age again affected much of Australia and the sedimentary rocks that formed during this time buried the Devonian reef. Deposition of sedimentary rocks in shallow seas and by rivers continued in the Canning and Bonaparte basins. Numerous diamond-bearing lamproite pipes were intruded into pre-existing rocks in the western Kimberley between 22 and 18 million years ago.

Diamonds from the Argyle mine

Photo - Courtesy of Argyle Diamonds

The landscape of the Kimberley is ancient and has been evolving for the last 250 million years. Over long periods of time, the effects of climate and erosion by water, wind and ice wears away hills and valleys and a nearly flat "planation" surface is produced, on which only isolated hills remain. If the surface is subsequently uplifted by earth movements, the landscape becomes rejuvenated, as rivers and streams cut down into and erode the old surface, forming a new system of hills and valleys. The presence of a former planation surface can usually be seen in the similar heights of hill tops within an area.

At least two planation surfaces formed in the Kimberley region, only to be eroded as the landscape was uplifted. Due to repeated uplifts, the oldest surface is now the highest, and is referred to as the High Kimberley surface. It was formed about 200 million years ago and is preserved only as remnants which are now the highest points of the main Kimberley Plateau. The tops of tablelands and mesas reach up to 776 metres above sea level at Mount Hann, before falling away to 200 to 300 metres along the coastline. The higher summits within the King Leopold and Durack Ranges (up to 937 metres at Mount Ord) originally formed remnant hills standing above this earliest surface.

Uplift and erosion of the High Kimberley surface took place between 200 and 100 million years ago and a new, lower planation surface, the Low Kimberley surface, formed around the main plateau, and originally extended over much of central and western Australia. A hard capping of laterite formed on the surface 70 to 50 million years ago. At that time Australia was in tropical latitudes, and the high rainfall caused deep weathering. Magnesium, calcium, sodium and potassium were leached from the surface rocks, concentrating iron and aluminium in the capping.

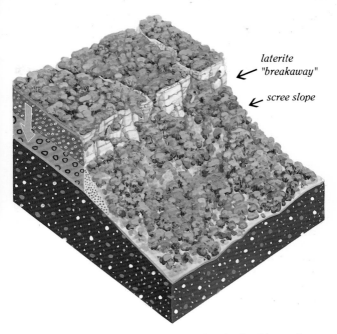

The Kimberley's Mitchell Plateau is capped with a hard layer of laterite, formed during a period of heavy tropical rainfall 70-50 million years ago

Thin soil cover

The "duricrust" of iron-rich caprock

The aluminium-rich bauxite layer

Rainwater leaches out magnesium, calcium, sodium and potassium atoms

Basal clay

Basalt bedrock

7

The present landscape of hills, valleys and gorges was produced by erosion that resulted from uplift of the Low Kimberley surface that started 20 million years ago, as Australia began to drift north towards Asia. The relief is still considerable and the landscape is a long way from the establishment of a new planation surface. The Low Kimberley surface is preserved around Halls Creek where, at between 500 and 600 metres above sea level, it divides the Ord River and the Fitzroy River drainage areas. The lower hill country (Bow River Hills, Halls Creek ridges, Lennard Hills and Napier Hills) around the edge of the Kimberley Plateau has been eroded from this surface, and this is reflected in the locally uniform level of the hill and ridge tops, which become progressively lower towards the coast. To the east and south-east of Halls Creek, the Duncan Highway and Tanami Road both climb out of the hill country onto plateau country covered by sandplains which form the Great Sandy and Tanami Deserts.

Rivers that originally meandered across the Low Kimberley surface have cut directly down into it as the surface was uplifted. As a result, the rivers' courses were not influenced by local geology, cutting directly through ridges of more resistant rocks, such as at Carlton Gorge, where the Ord River has cut through the Carr Boyd Ranges (see pages 30-31), rather than take an easier course around the north-eastern end of the range.

A rise in sea level about 17,000 years ago, following the last ice age, drowned the Kimberley coastline, with the sea now filling what were once river valleys. The Fitzroy River floodplain and the Cambridge Gulf Lowlands, which form the floodplain of the Ord River, started to form at this time. To complete the picture we see today, a more recent uplift resulted in the rivers and streams, which usually flow only after heavy rain during the cyclone season, cutting down below the level of their floodplains.

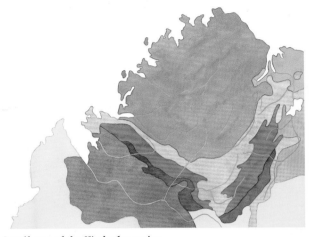

Landforms of the Kimberley region

- Cambridge Gulf lowlands
- Fitzroy floodplain
- Sandplain and desert
- Napier Hills (Devonian barrier reef)
- Ord Plain
- Granite country - Lennard and Bow River Hills
- Gold country - Halls Creek ridges
- Kimberley Foreland - King Leopold and Durack Ranges
- Kimberley Plateau

SEQUENCE OF GEOLOGICAL EVENTS

WEST KIMBERLEY

drowning of the coastline

uplift and erosion

Mount North lamproite

laterite formation - the Low Kimberley surface

CANNING BASIN

dinosaur footprints

formation of High Kimberley surface (Kimberley Plateau)

glacial rocks

barrier reef complex

period of major earth movements

glacial rocks

period of major earth movements

KIMBERLEY BASIN

dolerite sills

Kimberley sandstones

Kimberley sandstones

HOOPER COMPLEX

period of major earth movements

granites, gabbros and volcanic rocks

period of major earth movements

metamorphosed volcanic and sedimentary rocks

EAST KIMBERLEY	millions of years
drowning of the coastline	0.017
uplift and erosion	5
	20
laterite formation - the Low Kimberley surface	70
uplift and erosion	100
	135
formation of High Kimberley surface (Kimberley Plateau)	200
ORD AND BONAPARTE BASINS	
	290
sandstones and conglomerates	375
shallow sea deposits	500
basaltic volcanoes	540
period of major earth movements	560
glacial rocks	600
period of major earth movements	1000
Argyle diamond pipe	1190
VICTORIA RIVER BASIN	
river delta and shallow sea deposits	1200
BIRRINDUDU BASIN	
sandstones and stromatolitic limestones	1600
KIMBERLEY BASIN	
dolerite sills	1800
Kimberley sandstones	
LAMBOO COMPLEX	
granites and gabbros	1835
period of major earth movements	
	1865-1850
	1865
volcanic and sedimentary rocks	1910-1840

Rocks are classified into three types, according to their origin.

IGNEOUS ROCKS have solidified from molten rock (magma) formed deep within the Earth, which then moves upwards along cracks and faults. It may break through the Earth's surface and pour out as lava-forming volcanic rocks, such as basalt or rhyolite. Pyroclastic deposits ("tuffs") are the accumulations of ash and other material (including pumice) produced by explosive volcanic eruptions. Magma that does not reach the Earth's surface is injected ("intruded") into pre-existing rocks. Just below the Earth's surface this may take place along cracks to form "dykes", or along layers in sedimentary rocks to form "sills". These rocks take longer to cool, and the mineral grains have time to grow larger, forming medium-grained rocks such as dolerite. Deeper in the Earth's crust, magma may accumulate in large chambers that act as feeders to volcanoes at the surface. Such bodies take a very long time to solidify, forming coarse-grained rocks such as granite or gabbro.

Photo - Tim Griffin

Granite

SEDIMENTARY ROCKS form when rocks are broken down by weathering and by the action of water, wind and ice. Fragments of rock are then transported by rivers, tides or currents, by the wind, or by glaciers and ice sheets to be deposited as sediments in river channels, floodplains, seas, oceans, lakes, deserts, or by retreating glaciers and ice sheets. These sediments may be then buried by succeeding layers and over time become hardened into solid rock. Rocks made up of boulders, cobbles and pebbles are called conglomerates, those made up of sand are sandstones, and those formed of silt and mud are siltstones, mudstones and shales. Sedimentary rocks also form by the accumulation of animal and plant remains, forming limestone or coal.

Sandstone

METAMORPHIC ROCKS are formed when igneous or sedimentary rocks are altered by heat and/or pressure: turning sandstone and mudstone into schist and gneiss; basalt into amphibolite; limestone into marble; and granite and gabbro into granitic gneiss, amphibolite and granulite. Metamorphism may come about when major earth movements bury rocks deep in the Earth's crust, or through heating next to an igneous intrusion. New minerals, such as garnet, grow as the rock recrystallises.

Andalusite schist

Photos - Ian Tyler

The Kimberley Plateau is a vast area of comparatively flat high country, interrupted by sandstone escarpments that may stretch for tens of kilometres. Some of the most spectacular form the Cockburn and Pentecost Ranges, south-west of Wyndham. The plateau forms the central part of the Kimberley region.

DESCRIPTION: Extensive rugged tablelands and mesas rise up to nearly 800 metres in the central part of the plateau and dip gently north and west towards the sea. They are fringed by steep escarpments up to 300 metres high, through which large rivers have cut steep-sided gorges. Broad valleys between the escarpments contain low, boulder-strewn hills.

ROCK TYPES: Between 1835 and 1790 million years ago, the rocks that form most of the Kimberley Plateau were deposited in the Kimberley Basin beneath shallow seas, and by large braided river systems. Thick beds of sandstone are interlayered with beds of pebble and boulder conglomerate, mudstone, shale, dolomite (a magnesium-rich form of limestone, which may contain stromatolites) and basalt. The sequence of sedimentary and volcanic rocks was intruded by dolerite, formed by molten rock being injected between the layers of sandstone to form thick sills.

LANDFORM FORMATION: The Kimberley Plateau is up to 250 million years old and was uplifted and eroded between 200 and 100 million years ago, and again between 70 and 50 million years ago. Rivers incised into the sandstones about 20 million years ago, producing deep gorges. The broad valleys between the sandstone escarpments are underlain by less resistant rocks such as basalt and dolerite, and mudstone, shale and dolomite.

NOTABLE FEATURES: Cross-bedding can often be seen within the sandstones. Steeply-dipping layers record the passage of dunes within a river bed, or across a sea floor. The shape of the cross-beds reveals the direction in which rivers or sea currents were flowing.

Above: *King George Falls*   Below: *Cockburn Range*

Photo - Ian Oswald-Jacobs

Photo - Chris Done

MITCHELL PLATEAU

The Mitchell Plateau lies 120 kilometres south-west of Kalumburu, and extends inland from Admiralty Gulf on the northern Kimberley coast. The Mitchell River flows northwards, carving gorges and waterfalls into the sandstone and along the margins of the plateau. Two of the most spectacular results of this erosion are the Mitchell Falls and Surveyors Pool and Falls, each with a deep gorge downstream.

DESCRIPTION: The Mitchell Plateau rises up to 370 metres above sea level, and slopes down gently to the coast. It consists of extensive flat-topped mesas and plateau country, fringed by complex escarpments. The plateau is surrounded by low, rounded hills, and rises 60 to 150 metres above the headwaters of the adjacent Mitchell and Lawley Rivers.

ROCK TYPES: The plateau is composed of laterite and lateritic bauxite (aluminium ore), which have attracted the interest of mining companies since the 1960s, though they are currently regarded as uneconomic. These rocks are formed in tropical latitudes, where high humidity and rainfall cause deep weathering of the basalt surface, leaching elements such as potassium, sodium, magnesium and calcium from the original rock, and leaving behind aluminium in the form of a mineral called gibbsite.

LANDFORM FORMATION: The laterite capping formed when Australia had a more tropical climate 70 to 50 million years ago. Uplift and erosion during the last 20 million years has caused the creeks and rivers to cut down into the old land surface, producing the current landscape.

NOTABLE FEATURES: Basalt, a dark fine-grained rock of volcanic origin, underlies most of the Mitchell Plateau. The flat-lying beds of basalt form prominent terraces on the headlands near the coast, and benches around flat-topped mesas. The

The Mitchell Falls

laterite has only formed on top of the basaltic volcanic rocks, which contain aluminium, and has not developed on top of adjacent sandstone, which are made up almost entirely of silica.

Travelling along the Duncan Highway east of Halls Creek, or along the last stretch of the Tanami Road before it joins the Great Northern Highway takes you across the Kimberley's gold country. Many small mines, such as those around Old Halls Creek, Mount Dockrell, Grants Patch and at Ruby Queen, continued to be worked intermittently after the initial gold rush in the 1880s. A new mine near Palm Spring uses new techniques developed during the 1980s for extracting gold from low grade deposits. Copper, lead and zinc mineralisation is also known.

DESCRIPTION: The country consists of rocky, steep-sided, spinifex-covered ridges and hills incised by many small creeks and larger rivers. The tops of the hills are generally between 500 and 600 metres above sea level, and local relief is about 200 metres.

ROCK TYPES: The gold mineralisation occurs within rocks known to geologists as the Halls Creek Group, a sequence of volcanic rocks (mainly basalt, with some trachyte and trachyandesite) and weakly metamorphosed sedimentary rocks (cobble and pebble conglomerate, pebbly sandstone, quartz sandstone, feldspathic sandstone, and mudstone) that is between 1920 and 1850 million years old.

LANDFORM FORMATION: The rocks are very old but the landscape is not, having been shaped by the rivers and creeks eroding down into an ancient land surface during the last 20 million years.

NOTABLE FEATURES: Quartz veins often occur, similar to that forming the China Wall near Halls Creek. Gold may occur within such veins, deposited from hot mineralising fluids flowing through cracks and faults in the rock. Gold also accumulates in the beds of streams and rivers that are eroding the quartz veins. Where the Duncan Highway crosses the Black Elvire River near Palm Spring,

Photo - Bill Belson

Above: *China Wall, a quartz vein near Halls Creek*

Right: *Old Ruby Queen gold mine*

Photo - Ian Tyler

the sandstones exposed in the river bed show deposition from currents loaded with suspended sediment. These flow down an underwater slope and spread out across a flat bed at the bottom. Deposition of the sandstone bed happens very quickly with the larger, heavier sediment grains settling first, while the finer grains settle later, on top (see sandstone photograph on page 13).

BOW RIVER TO DUFFER RANGE

The core of an ancient mountain range

Hill country that stretches for about 130 kilometres on either side of the Great Northern Highway, between the Bow River and the Duffer Range, is formed by rocks known collectively as the Tickalara Metamorphics. They were formed 1850 million years ago when the original rocks were transformed - or metamorphosed - under intense pressure and heat inside a mountain range, up to 25 kilometres beneath the Earth's surface. Sandstone and mudstone became schist and gneiss; basalt lava became amphibolite; limestone was transformed into marble; while granite and gabbro became granitic gneiss, amphibolite and granulite.

DESCRIPTION: The Tickalara Metamorphics form rugged, boulder-strewn hills and plateau country. In places, they reach more than 500 metres above sea level. The hills are traversed by small creeks and larger rivers, with relief of up to 250 metres.

ROCK TYPES: Rocks include schists, gneisses, amphibolites, marbles, granitic gneiss and granulite. Metamorphic minerals include staurolite, garnet, muscovite and biotite mica, cordierite, sillimanite, andalusite, spinel, wollastonite, scapolite, epidote, amphibole and pyroxene.

NOTABLE FEATURES: The Spring Creek track into Purnululu National Park crosses the Tickalara Metamorphics. The Mabel Downs Tonalite, which was injected into the metamorphic rocks 1830 million years ago, before being deformed with them, can be seen in a creek crossing soon after leaving the Great Northern Highway. It is a medium-grained, grey rock with a well-developed alignment of the dark minerals (biotite and amphibole) found within it. It contains angular pieces of the older Tickalara Metamorphics, which were pulled off the walls of the intrusion as the magma was injected, a process known as "stoping". Further east, the track winds through the Tickalara Metamorphics and passes an outcrop of marble which shows spectacular folding.

Photo - Ian Tyler

Above: *Migmatite*   Below: *The Tickalara Metamorphics (the hills)*

Photo - Ian Oswald-Jacobs

In steep creeks, west of the Warmun rubbish tip, outcrops show spectacular evidence of the Tickalara Metamorphics beginning to melt as temperatures reached 800°C. Such rocks are known as migmatites (literally "mixed rock") and these examples contain numerous lumps of rock that did not reach their melting point. Large garnet crystals can be seen in the migmatite.

The 15,000 square kilometre area around the edge of the Kimberley Plateau is dominated by granite outcrops. In the western Kimberley, the Gibb River Road winds through this country, between the Devonian reef and the King Leopold Ranges. In the eastern Kimberley, it lies mostly to the west of the Great Northern Highway, although the road passes through it north of the Bow River.

DESCRIPTION: Rounded tors (hills made up of jumbled blocks of rock), and boulder-strewn "whalebacks" reach up to 630 metres above sea level. Areas underlain by volcanic rocks are characterised by low, rounded hills. Local relief is in the order of 150 metres, with the intervening creeks and rivers occupying broad sandy valleys. Boab trees often grow along the creeks.

ROCK TYPES: The main rock types are varieties of grey and pink granite between 1865 and 1800 million years old. They consist of varying amounts of the minerals quartz, plagioclase feldspar, potassium feldspar, biotite mica and amphibole. Mixed in with the granites are large areas of dark green to black gabbro, made up of the minerals olivine, pyroxene, amphibole, plagioclase feldspar, and biotite mica. The granites are interspersed with volcanic rocks of a similar age that reached the Earth's surface to form rhyolite and rhyodacite lava flows, or pyroclastic rocks that were produced by violent volcanic eruptions.

LANDFORM FORMATION: The landforms have been eroded by rivers and creeks in the last 20 million years. In massive rock units, such as granites, weathering and erosion is controlled by the patterns of regular cracks, or joints, within them. Tors generally form where the joints are quite closely spaced, whereas whalebacks develop where the joints are very widely spaced, so that each represents a huge single granite block.

NOTABLE FEATURES: Granites are usually coarse-grained rocks. often containing scattered crystals of feldspar that are much larger

Above: *Typical "whaleback"*　　　　　Below: *Granite tor*

Photo - Ian Oswald-Jacobs

Photo - Tim Griffin

than other crystals nearby (see photo on page 12). This texture is thought to form if the magma moved from deep in the Earth's crust, where it was cooling slowly and growing large crystals, to a level higher in the crust, where it cooled more rapidly, so that the remaining liquid formed smaller crystals. The granites in the western Kimberley have been quarried as an ornamental facing stone known as 'Kimberley Pearl'.

The McIntosh Hills, between the Panton and Ord Rivers, are a spectacular sight from the air, as their semi-circular and circular structure can clearly be seen. Watch out for them if you take a scenic flight from Halls Creek to Purnululu National Park.

DESCRIPTION: The hills form a series of semi-circular and circular, spinifex-covered, boulder-strewn ridges, which rise 150 metres from the intervening valleys to reach up to 567 metres above sea level.

ROCK TYPES: The rocks that form the hills are rich in iron, magnesium and calcium. They include peridotite, made up of the minerals olivine and pyroxene; varieties of gabbro, made up of varying amounts of the minerals olivine, pyroxene, magnetite, amphibole, plagioclase feldspar and biotite mica; and anorthosite, made up almost entirely of plagioclase feldspar with some pyroxene.

LANDFORM FORMATION: The hills have been eroded during the last 20 million years. Each ridge is made up of layers of rock, usually gabbro, which are more resistant to weathering and erosion, while those forming the valleys have eroded more quickly.

NOTABLE FEATURES: The most obvious feature of the McIntosh Hills is their circular form. The rocks are part of a large layered intrusion, which formed 1830 million years ago with the injection of several pulses of molten rock (magma) of different composition into a large chamber of magma; each pulse crystallising as a separate layer. The layers dip inwards and become shallower towards the centre of the structure, so that the intrusion is saucer-shaped, with the conduit that fed magma into it being under the centre.

Photo - Ian Oswald-Jacobs

The McIntosh intrusion is the best preserved of a number of layered intrusions in the eastern Kimberley that are between 1860 and 1830 million years old. It is a good prospect for economic deposits of chrome, platinum and nickel mineralisation.

KING LEOPOLD AND DURACK RANGES

The King Leopold Ranges and the Durack Range extend for some 600 kilometres along the south-western and eastern edges of the Kimberley Plateau, from Walcott Inlet in the north-west Kimberley to Kununurra in the north-east.

DESCRIPTION: The ranges consist of long, rugged, spinifex-covered ridges and escarpments. Mount Ord, in the King Leopold Ranges, reaches 937 metres above sea level, making it the highest point in the Kimberley. The sides of the valleys are generally steep and have only a thin soil cover supporting sparse vegetation, or are nearly vertical with precipitous bare rock cliffs. In places, the ranges are cut by steep-sided gorges up to 300 metres deep. The ridge tops stand up to 600 metres above the valleys.

ROCK TYPES: The ridges are composed of white to pale brown cross-bedded sandstone, and pebble and cobble conglomerate deposited in the Kimberley Basin (see page 14). Outcrops in the valleys are of less resistant mudstone, siltstone, shale, dolomite and basalt, together with sills of dark grey dolerite formed by the injection of molten rocks between the layers of sedimentary rock.

LANDFORM FORMATION: The King Leopold and Durack Ranges are the margins of the Kimberley Plateau. The highest summits formed as isolated hills (monadnocks), before uplift and erosion took place between 200 and 100 million years ago and 70 to 50 million years ago. The present landscape of valleys, ridges and deep gorges developed after uplift began 20 million years ago.

NOTABLE FEATURES: At Inglis Gap, where the Gibb River Road winds its way into the King Leopold Range, sandstone and pebble conglomerate exposed in the walls lie over granite. This contact represents a gap in the local geological record of 15 to 20 million years (although rocks that formed during this period are preserved elsewhere). Geologists refer to such a break in the sequence of rocks as an "unconformity".

Dramatic folding in sandstone beds in the King Leopold Range

Photo - Ian Oswald-Jacobs

South-east of Mount Bell, the road makes an abrupt turn beneath a cliff more than 50 metres high, in which tightly folded beds of sandstone are exposed. Folding and faulting can also be seen in the walls of Lennard River Gorge. These structures were formed about 560 million years ago during a period of mountain building, when the edges of the Kimberley Basin were crumpled as it was pushed to the south-west, over the underlying granite.

The Osmond Range lies to the north of Purnululu National Park and its structure of broad, open folds can be seen on scenic flights from Kununurra and Warmun.

DESCRIPTION: High ridges and escarpments up to 700 metres above sea level are characterised by curving, mostly northerly and north-easterly dipping, rugged, spinifex-covered slopes. Relief of up to 400 metres occurs in the western end of the range.

ROCK TYPES: In the central part of the Osmond Range, granite and gabbro intruded into metamorphosed sandstone, mudstone and dolomite, probably related to the Tickalara Metamorphics (see page 20). These rocks are overlain by sandstone, conglomerate and basalt, similar to those in the Kimberley Basin to the west. The main range is made up of a sequence of sandstone and conglomerate, interlayered with mudstone, shale, siltstone and dolomite. The lowermost sandstone and overlying dolomite may have been deposited about 1400 million years ago; while the overlying sandstone and siltstone may have been deposited between 1200 and 800 million years ago.

LANDFORM FORMATION: The ridges are formed by hard, resistant sandstone, while the creeks and rivers follow the less resistant beds of dolomite, mudstone, siltstone and shale.

NOTABLE FEATURES: The rocks forming the Osmond Range have a distinctively curved outcrop pattern due to being folded by major earth movements. The movements last occurred around 370 million years ago and caused uplift and then erosion. Overall, the rocks form an arch-like structure, or anticline, which plunges beneath the surface towards the north-east, with older rocks forming the core of the structure in the western part of the range. A similar structure, formed by the same succession of rocks, is repeated to the north of the Osmond Fault. Many beds within the dolomite are full of fossil stromatolites; domes, cones or columns

Above: *The broad, open folds typical of the Osmond Range*

Right: *Fossil stromatolites from the Osmond Range*

built up of successive layers of what was originally calcium carbonate deposited by cyanobacteria. Similar forms are growing today at Shark Bay.

CARR BOYD RANGES

The Carr Boyd Ranges, south of Kununurra, lie north and west of Lake Argyle. The Argyle Dam has been built at the head of Carlton Gorge, cut by the Ord River through the northern part of the ranges.

DESCRIPTION: The Carr Boyd Ranges reach up to 560 metres above sea level, and are made up of a series of escarpments and north-westerly dipping slopes, cut by steep-sided valleys and gorges up to 200 metres deep. The northern and southern ranges are separated by a broad valley, containing low rocky hills, and occupied by the headwaters of Revolver Creek.

ROCK TYPES: Sandstones, siltstones, mudstones and shales were deposited by a river delta and beneath a shallow sea 1200 million years ago, and form what is known collectively as the Carr Boyd Group. Beneath it is the Revolver Creek Formation, comprised of sandstone, siltstone and basalt. Granite, gabbro, volcanic rocks and metasedimentary rocks, typical of the granite country, occur around the headwaters of Revolver Creek, along the western shore of Lake Argyle, and north-east of the dam.

LANDFORM FORMATION: Creeks and rivers have cut down into the Low Kimberley surface, eroding out the Carr Boyd Ranges 20 million years ago. Uplift at that time caused the Ord River to cut down into the sandstones to form Carlton Gorge.

NOTABLE FEATURES: Along Carlton Gorge, the succession of sedimentary rocks that make up the Carr Boyd Group dip to the north. They were deposited on the sea floor as flat beds, but have been tilted by later earth movements. The rocks near the dam are the oldest, with each overlying bed becoming successively younger.

In the narrowest part of the gorge, a succession of depositional cycles are exposed in the walls, reflecting repeated deepening, then shallowing along the shoreline of an ancient

Above: *The Carr Boyd Ranges*   Below: *The walls of Carlton Gorge*

Photo - Chris Done

Photo - Alan Thorne

sea. Each cycle consists of red to brown siltstone, that was deposited in the sea, beneath white quartz sandstone, that was deposited when a river delta built out over the siltstone.

In 1979, two diamonds were discovered in gravel in Smoke Creek, 110 kilometres south-west of Kununurra, the result of a program of systematic exploration that began in 1972. The discovery of more diamonds upstream eventually led the exploration team to the Argyle Pipe, which lies exposed on a ridge at the end of the Matsu Range. The body, about 1600 metres long, and from 600 to 150 metres wide, is the richest diamond pipe in the world, with a grade of four and a half carats per tonne. Fifty five per cent of the diamonds are used in jewellery and 45 per cent are of industrial quality. Gem quality diamonds include champagne and pink varieties. Variations in colour can be caused by gases and impurities trapped in the diamond during formation. Pink diamonds are thought to be coloured by stress and twisting in the crystal lattice. Mining began in 1985, and the Argyle diamond mine is now the world's largest producer of natural diamonds, with a third of the world supply. The mine can be seen from the Great Northern Highway near the Bow River crossing, and is a feature of scenic flights from Kununurra to Purnululu National Park. The mine is open for tours.

ROCK TYPES: The Argyle Pipe intruded into sedimentary rocks 1200 million years ago, and is composed of an unusual igneous rock called olivine lamproite, made up of the minerals olivine, pyroxene, phlogopite, leucite, amphibole and potassium feldspar.

FORMATION AND DISTINCTIVE GEOLOGICAL FEATURES: Diamonds are formed when carbon is subjected to very high pressures deep within the Earth. The magma forming the Argyle Pipe was produced by melting in the mantle 150 kilometres beneath the Earth's surface. At the pressures at such depths diamonds are stable and were included in the magma, which then moved rapidly upwards through cracks and faults into the crust. As the magma neared the surface, dissolved gases such as steam and carbon

Photo - Courtesy of Argyle Diamonds

dioxide came out of solution as the pressure on it dropped (just as gas bubbles out of a fizzy drink bottle if you shake it and remove the cap). Groundwater within the sandstones also turned rapidly into steam. The resulting explosion shattered the overlying rock, fragments of which were then incorporated into the magma, producing distinctive rocks (sandy tuffs, which are essentially consolidated volcanic ash combined with the sandstone fragments), as well as lavas.

NOTE: Similar intrusions in the western Kimberley are only 20 to 18 million years old, and some are known to contain diamonds. One intrusion forms Mount North, south-west of Windjana Gorge.

GLACIAL DEPOSITS

Louisa Downs Station to the State border

Glaciers are essentially large "rivers" of ice that are moving forward very very slowly, under the weight of fresh falls of snow at their "head". They are usually found in mountainous areas or in polar regions. While it is hard to imagine today, about 600 million years ago the Kimberley was in the grip of a major ice age. Glaciers once descended from either side of a range of ice-capped mountains, which probably stretched from the Northern Territory border to Louisa Downs Station. The glacial deposits from the eastern side of this ancient range can be seen along the last part of the Spring Creek Track, west of the Purnululu ranger station, and along the Duncan Highway east of Palm Spring. The western deposits are exposed around Louisa Downs Station between Halls Creek and Fitzroy Crossing, and on Mount House Station east of the Gibb River Road.

ROCK TYPES: If you visit a modern glacier, such as the Franz Josef Glacier in New Zealand, you would see a chaotic jumble of pebbles, cobbles and boulders that have been deposited by the melting ice at its foot. Glaciers are an amazing force in sculpting the landscape. The enormous weight and force of the moving ice tears away rocks of varying sizes from the valley floor and walls and may redeposit them hundreds of kilometres from their source. These deposits are known as moraine or till, and when they are compacted together they form a sedimentary rock known as tillite. Tillite is exposed in a road cutting 75 kilometres west of Halls Creek, where it lies on granite. Glaciation was followed by rising sea levels as the ice sheets melted and the tillites are overlain by layers of sandstone, siltstone, mudstone, shale and stromatolitic dolomite deposited in shallow seas.

NOTABLE FEATURES: As glaciers move across rock outcrops, the ice scours them to produce a polished surface, into which stones embedded in the ice etch grooves. Such glacial pavements

Tillite deposits

Photo - Ian Tyler

Ice-capped mountains spanned the Kimberley 600 million years ago

can be seen at Pavement Hill, north of Louisa Downs Station, and near Mount House Station. The smoothed side of the pavement faces the direction from which the ice came.

Zebra rock, a sedimentary rock with distinctive spots and stripes, occurs within siltstones overlying the tillites east of Kununurra. The patterning probably formed during the process that hardened the sediment into solid rock, and may reflect the different oxidation states of iron within the sediment.

Ice-scoured glacial pavement near Mount House Station

Photo - Ian Tyler

For the past 1800 million years, a rigid piece of ancient continental crust, which probably formed more than 2500 million years ago, has been buried beneath the Kimberley Basin. During that time, little deformation has affected the overlying sandstone rocks. However, earth movements around its edges have caused it and the overlying sedimentary rocks to flex, creating an extensive system of cracks and joints. Bell Creek Gorge has been carved out along the line of one of these cracks.

DESCRIPTION: You approach Bell Creek Gorge from the Gibb River Road through the low rounded hills within the Silent Grove valley. The valley sides are rugged, spinifex-covered slopes that reach more than 350 metres up to Mount Chalmer (704 metres above sea level), to the south-west, and Mount Frank (649 metres), to the north-east. At the head of the valley, Bell Creek drops 150 metres into a gorge and continues north-west to join the Isdell River.

ROCK TYPES: The valley floor is formed by basalt lavas interbedded with sandstones, mudstones and shales, while the surrounding hills and the waterfall at the head of the gorge are sandstone. Cutting through the sedimentary and volcanic rocks is a wall-like intrusion of dolerite, known as a "dyke", which cuts across the layering of pre-existing rocks. The dyke was formed by the injection of magma along a vertical crack or joint, between 560 and 500 million years ago. Dolerite, a medium-grained version of basalt, contains the minerals olivine, pyroxene and plagioclase.

LANDFORM FORMATION: The valley and gorge were eroded during uplift and erosion 20 million years ago. Bell Creek carved out its gorge by following the less resistant dolerite through the sandstone. Further to the north-west, the dyke has controlled the course of the Isdell River.

NOTABLE FEATURES: The dolerite forming the dyke is exposed as two boulder-strewn hills at the head of the Silent Grove valley,

Photo - Carolyn Thomson

and can be traced from the granite country to the coast at Doubtful Bay, a distance of more than 175 kilometres.

The basalts within the valley occupy the core of a syncline (a fold shaped like an inverted arch), where the sandstones forming the valley sides have buckled to dip inwards to form a trough-shape that plunges beneath the surface to the south-east. The overlying sandstone forms the prominent escarpment of Rifle Point. On a much smaller scale, the sandstone at the top of the waterfall forms an anticline (an arch-like structure, and therefore the opposite to a syncline).

ORD PLAINS

Ancient lava flows and former seas

The best cattle grazing country in the eastern Kimberley is on the Ord Plains, south and east of Lake Argyle and south-east of Purnululu National Park. Between 560 and 530 million years ago, these areas were awash with flows of molten lava that erupted from fissures and spread out for several tens of kilometres. From 540 to 500 million years ago, in Cambrian times, the hardened lavas were covered with shallow seas, during a time when the diversity of life on Earth exploded. Fossils in the limestone rocks laid down in these seas include stromatolites, trilobites and brachiopods.

DESCRIPTION: The countryside is a dissected plateau, reaching up to 450 metres above sea level, covered with extensive grasslands and woodlands and interspersed with low, boulder-strewn hills and mesas. Numerous creeks have carved out gullies and small gorges, and the main rivers have cut gorges up to 100 metres deep. The plateau country merges downslope into broad, featureless, grass-covered plains of black soil.

ROCK TYPES: Extensive flows of basalt lava, known as the Antrim Plateau Volcanics, vary from four metres to more than 100 metres thick. The basalt is overlain by limestone, sandstone and mudstone which originated beneath the former sea.

LANDFORM FORMATION: The plateau country was uplifted some 20 million years ago, and was then incised by creeks and rivers.

NOTABLE FEATURES: Sections through individual lava flows can be seen in the sides of gorges, often separated by deposits of sandstone, siltstone, limestone and chert. The basalt contains numerous holes called "vesicles", which represent gas bubbles frozen into the lava as it cooled, and those at the bottom may be pipe-like. These holes were sometimes filled by calcite or quartz during a later period. Large vesicles may contain agate, consisting of innumerable thin, multicoloured bands of quartz.

Flat-lying basalt lava flows can be seen at Nicholson Gorge on the Ord Plains

Evidence of the shallow nature of the seas is provided by extensive ripple marks, formed by waves, preserved on the tops of the sandstone beds. Tracks, trails and burrows record the movements of animals across and through the former sea floor.

GEIKIE GORGE AND WINDJANA GORGE

The Devonian Barrier Reef

A "Great Barrier Reef" fringed an ancient Kimberley land mass during the Devonian period, between 375 and 350 million years ago, when a tropical sea filled the Canning and Bonaparte Basins. Remnants of the reef are preserved in the western Kimberley as ranges of low, rugged hills extending for 350 kilometres along the edge of the granite country, parallel to the King Leopold Ranges. The reef probably extended for more than 1000 kilometres around the seaward margin of the Kimberley and is also seen north of Kununurra, where it forms the Ningbing Range. The reefs were built by lime-secreting organisms, mainly calcareous bacteria and extinct coral-like organisms called stromatoporoids. Though corals were present, they were much less important in reef-building than the corals of modern times. Gastropods, brachiopods, bivalves, fish and stromatolites were also present in and around the reef.

DESCRIPTION: The ancient reef now forms a chain of often steep-sided ranges, up to 300 metres above sea level, that include the Napier, Oscar, Pillara and Emanuel Ranges. Higher (up to 360 metres above sea level), rounded, sandstone and conglomerate hills form the Van Emmerick, Barramundi and Sparke Ranges, as well as Mount Behn. The limestone ranges rise from 40 to 150 metres above the surrounding Fitzroy River floodplain. The Lennard and Fitzroy Rivers have cut through the ranges to form Windjana and Geikie gorges.

ROCK TYPES: The ancient reef is mostly limestone (consisting largely of calcium carbonate), with lesser amounts of mudstone, sandstone and conglomerate. The rocks contain fossils of the plants and animals that lived on and around the reef. Deposits of sandstone and pebble, cobble and boulder conglomerate occur at intervals along the barrier reef. In the Canning Basin the reef is overlain by mudstone, limestone and sandstone deposited after the reefs became extinct, about 250 million years ago.

Photo - Carolyn Thomson

Geikie Gorge

43

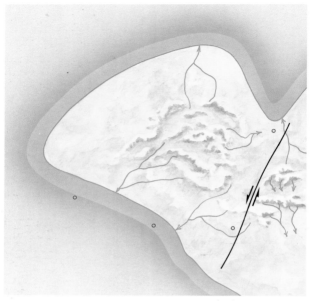

The Kimberley as it was thought to look around 350 million years ago

LANDFORM FORMATION: The formation of the present landscape occurred in two stages. The first took place 250 million years ago when the reef was uplifted above sea level and eroded. Some caves in the limestone formed at this time. The reef was then buried by younger sedimentary rocks. When the whole area began to be uplifted and eroded 20 million years ago, the limestone forming the reef was more resistant to erosion than the overlying rocks, so that the ancient landscape was exhumed from beneath them. The reef now stands above the surrounding plains, much as it would have stood above the sea floor 350 million years ago.

NOTABLE FEATURES: Cross-sections through the barrier reef can be seen in the walls of Windjana and Geikie Gorges. In such places, you can see where flat-lying limestone beds adjoin steeply dipping beds. The flat-lying beds are the back-reef limestones, laid down within protected lagoons between the reef and the shore. The front of the reef, which faced the sea, is marked by the steeply dipping limestones. These were underwater scree slopes formed by the accumulation of debris eroded by waves from the reef top. In places large, jumbled blocks of reef limestone can be seen on these slopes. Fossil sponges, brachiopods, nautiloids and stromatolites may be found in the slope deposits.

Photo - Phillip Playford

This photograph of Windjana Gorge clearly shows the structure of the former barrier reef in cross-section

A reconstruction of the reef, as it would have looked in Devonian times, 350 million years ago

Around the reef, mudstones, sandstones and thin limestones represent material deposited in the deeper and quieter waters of the basin floor adjacent to the reef. Here, fossil ammonoids (shelled animals that are now extinct), nautiloids and more than 25 species of the prehistoric, armour-plated fish (the Gogo fish), that dominated Devonian times, may be found. Fish were the first vertebrates and some species eventually developed rudimentary limbs and the ability to breathe air, becoming the precursors to the amphibians, reptiles, mammals and birds.The Tunnel Creek-Windjana Gorge Road passes through the reef limestones and around the south-eastern end of the Oscar Range and back onto limestone, some 10 kilometres from the Great Northern Highway turn-off. The core of the Oscar Range is formed of rock more than 600 million years old, and was an offshore island in the Devonian sea, fringed by the reef.

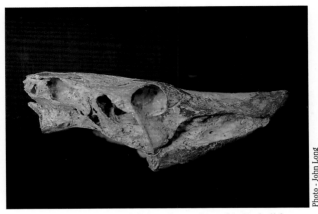

Above: *Late Devonian lungfish (*Griphognathus whitei*) skull from near Windjana Gorge*

Below: *A reconstruction of the fish*

At the time the reef was forming, the interior of the ancient Kimberley land mass was being drained by torrential rivers. Their channels continued offshore and the deposits of sandstone and conglomerate, such as those at Mount Behn, show where they passed through the reef.

Numerous caves are found within the limestone forming the Devonian reef. The best known is at Tunnel Creek, 30 kilometres south-east of Windjana Gorge. The Aboriginal leader Jandamarra used Tunnel Creek as a hideout from the Police for many years, and was killed near its entrance in 1897.

DESCRIPTION: Tunnel Creek can be followed for 750 metres from one side of the Napier Range to the other. The roof has collapsed through to the top of the range near the centre of the tunnel. An intricate network of narrow caves and open fissures has formed where Mimbi Creek flows through the southern end of the Lawford Range. These fascinating caves occur just north of the Great Northern Highway, 80 kilometres south-east of Fitzroy Crossing.

LANDFORM FORMATION: Limestone is made up of calcium carbonate, which is readily dissolved by slightly acidic rainwater seeping from the land surface into the rock. Over many thousands of years, water flowing along cracks, joints and bedding surfaces dissolves the limestone away, opening them out to form caves. Cave systems have formed whenever the reef has been exposed at the Earth's surface. This first occurred 250 million years ago, and some of the present cave systems may have originated at that time. These were rejuvenated over the past 20 million years as the reefs were exhumed.

NOTABLE FEATURES: Tunnel Creek follows a prominent joint or fault, which has acted as a channel for groundwater flowing through the limestone, and eroding out the tunnel. The caves at Mimbi Creek have formed from the erosion of a prominent system of joints in the limestone, which intersect each other at right angles. An intricate system of high, narrow, interconnected passageways is the result. The presence of underground pools along the floors of the caves is due to the water table (the level

Mimbi Caves

to which rock beneath the surface is saturated with ground water) being just at the present erosion surface. Water only flows through the caves after prolonged heavy rain during the wet season. During the dry season, water dripping from the roof of the caves and onto the floor precipitates calcite to form stalactitites and stalagmites, or flows down the walls to form curtains of flowstone.

Devonian sandstones

Sandstones and conglomerates, with distinctive beehive-shaped towers, now form the Bungle Bungle and Dixon Ranges in Purnululu National Park, the Ragged Range to the north of the Argyle Diamond Mine, and Hidden Valley at Kununurra. These sedimentary formations were deposited into the Ord and Bonaparte Basins, 375 to 350 million years ago, when the Halls Creek Fault system was active in the eastern Kimberley (see page 56).

DESCRIPTION: The Bungle Bungle Range reaches up to 578 metres above sea level. The range stands 200 to 300 metres above a woodland and grass-covered plain, with steep cliffs forming its western face. Elsewhere, particularly where Piccaninny Creek cuts into the range to form Piccaninny Gorge, the range is cut by deep gullies and breaks up into complex areas of ridges and beehive-shaped towers with distinctive orange and black or grey bands.

Similar towers, pinnacles and ridges, reaching up to 569 metres above sea level, form the Blatchford Escarpment along the western edge of the Ragged Range. Lower, less well-developed towers and ridges form Kelly's Knob and Mount Cyril in Hidden Valley National Park at Kununurra.

ROCK TYPES: The Bungle Bungle and Dixon Ranges are formed by quartz sandstone and conglomerate, with some siltstone. The Ragged Range is dominated by sandstone and conglomerate, while Hidden Valley consists of quartz sandstone and conglomerate, with dolomitic sandstone, dolomite, mudstone and siltstone.

LANDFORM FORMATION: The distinctive beehive-shaped landforms have been produced by uplift and erosion during the last 20 million years. Before that time, however, the rocks had been subjected to deep weathering typical of tropical climates. As a result, laterite formed a hard cap on the surface 70 to 50 million years ago. This deep weathering weakened the sandstones and

Above: *The Bungle Bungle*   Below: *Large-scale cross-bedding*

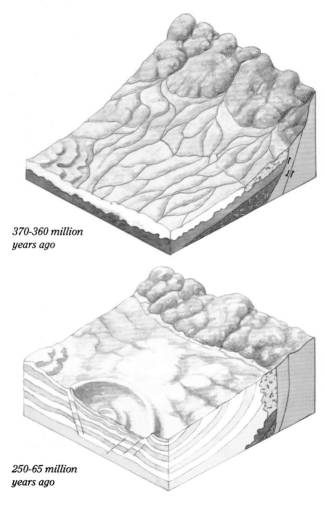

*370-360 million
years ago*

*250-65 million
years ago*

52

Present day

made them friable, by dissolving the silica cement that binds the sand grains together. The weight of overlying rocks still holds the sand grains in place, but when this is removed, the sandstones are easily eroded and the rounded tops reflect this lack of internal strength. The flow of water over the surface is concentrated by any further weakness or irregularities in the rock, such as cracks or joints, and rapidly erodes the narrow channels that separate the towers.

NOTABLE FEATURES: An obvious feature of the sandstones, particularly in the Bungle Bungle Range, is the prominent orange and black or grey banding. More permeable (which means that water is able to move through it with relative ease) layers of rock allow moisture to seep through to the rock surface, promoting a dark cyanobacterial growth. In between, the less permeable layers are covered with a patina of iron and manganese staining. These outer coatings (the rock beneath is a whitish colour) help to protect the lower parts of the towers from erosion.

At the time the sandstones and conglomerates were deposited, active faults were altering the landscape. To the north of what is now the Bungle Bungle Range, uplift occurred along the Osmond Fault in the Osmond Range, and to the west took place along the Halls Creek Fault. Uplift of the Carr Boyd Ranges took place to the east of the present day Ragged Range, along the Revolver Creek Fault, and to the south-east of what is now Hidden Valley, again along the Halls Creek Fault. Streams and rivers eroded these ancient highlands and at their edges slopes were steep and the energy in the streams and rivers was high, allowing them to carry large boulders. As the steepness of the slopes decreased, the streams and rivers had less energy and boulder conglomerates, which can be seen in the Ragged Range or in the walls of Echidna Chasm, were deposited. Some of the boulders at Echidna Chasm show scratches and grooves typical of erosion by ice, as they were eroded out of the glacial rocks exposed in the Osmand Range, only to be redeposited a few kilometres further south. However, most of the rocks in the Bungle Bungle Range and at Hidden Valley are sandstones deposited further from the highlands by lower energy braided rivers flowing across broad plains in open valleys.

The sandstones show well-developed cross-bedding, which records the passage of dunes within the bed of the rivers. The direction in which the rivers were flowing can be established from the shape of the dunes. Cross-bedded sandstones that formed from windblown sand dunes have also been recognised.

Right: *The walls of Echidna Chasm are made up of conglomerates*

Photo - Chris Done

THE HALLS CREEK FAULT SYSTEM

A major fracture in the Earth's crust, on the scale of the San Andreas Fault, extends for more than 850 kilometres through the eastern Kimberley and into the Northern Territory, stretching from the edge of the Great Sandy Desert to Darwin. While it is not presently active, it has had a complex history of vertical and horizontal movement over the past 1830 million years.

DESCRIPTION: Sandstone cliffs and steep scree slopes, nearly 300 metres high, form an escarpment marking the Halls Creek Fault at the western end of the Osmond Range, and similar escarpments mark the position of other faults through the sandstones of the Durack and Carr Boyd Ranges. Where faults cut granites and gabbros, or metamorphosed sedimentary rocks, they may be marked by lower escarpments (up to 100 metres high), or prominent ridges trending north to north-easterly.

ROCK TYPES: The faults may be marked by quartz veins (like the one forming the China Wall) that follow zones of shattered and fractured rock (like breaking toffee that has cooled and hardened). Some faults formed deep within the Earth's crust, where the rocks tend to flow rather than break (like stretching warm toffee), resulting in highly flattened and stretched rocks called "mylonites".

LANDFORM FORMATION: The escarpments along the Halls Creek Fault mark a change in rock type across the fault, with the more resistant rocks on one side of the fault standing up as cliffs or higher hills. Where the fault is within a single rock type, zones of quartz veining, which are more resistant to erosion, stand up as ridges. This is the case near Old Halls Creek.

NOTABLE FEATURES: The Halls Creek Fault is part of a system of wrench faults on which movement was horizontal, similar to the San Andreas Fault in California. The rocks on the western side of the fault system have slid to the left (south-west), relative

Satellite imagery clearly shows the Halls Creek Fault trending north to north-easterly

Photo - Courtesy of Argyle Diamonds

The Argyle Diamond Mine - the Halls Creek Fault may have provided a pathway from deep within the Earth, along which diamond-rich magma reached the surface

to those on the eastern side, and it is referred to as a "sinistral" (left-handed) fault system.

The fault system has moved several times since the Kimberley was joined to the rest of northern Australia, and movement may have coincided with folding at the edge of the Kimberley Basin, in the western Kimberley, 560 million years ago. Accumulated movements of between 100 and 200 kilometres have been suggested along the faults. The present fault pattern cuts the Devonian sandstones, and was active at least 350 million years ago, a time when major earth movements were taking place in central Australia.

Photo - Ian Oswald-Jacobs

Escarpment of the Halls Creek Fault at Calico Spring

DINOSAUR FOOTPRINTS

Although much of the Kimberley region has remained above sea level for the last 250 million years, the deposition of sedimentary rock in shallow seas and by rivers continued to the south-west, within the Canning Basin. Around 135 million years ago, during the early Cretaceous period, the area around Broome consisted of tidal flats, and these were crossed by what is thought to have been a large meat-eating dinosaur (*Megalosauropus broomensis*). Trails of footprints occur on the nearly horizontal, ripple-marked surfaces of several beds of cross-bedded, reddish sandstone and siltstone, within what is now the Broome Sandstone (see photo on page 71).

Several groups of dinosaur footprints are known, and the best preserved is a group of ten prints occurring about 50 metres seaward (south-west) of cliffs near the lighthouse at Gantheaume Point. The footprints are normally covered by the sea and can be seen only during very low tides.

The footprints themselves are three-toed, up to 50 centimetres long, and appear to have been made by more than one individual. One trackway consists of four prints, two from each foot, indicating that the dinosaur had a stride of about two metres.

Since their initial discovery in the 1950s, many more types of dinosaur footprints were identified in the 1990s. It is now believed that at least seven different types of dinosaurs existed in the region during the early Cretaceous period. These included large long-necked sauropods, bipedal plant-eating ornithischians, small carnivorous theropods and possibly stegosaurs. Current research on Broome dinosaur trackways is being carried out by the Western Australian Museum to identify, catalogue and cast representative footprints of each of the dinosaur families.

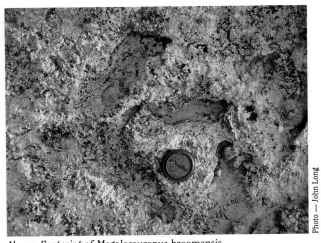

Above: *Footprint of* Megalosauropus broomensis
Below: *A reconstruction of the dinosaur*

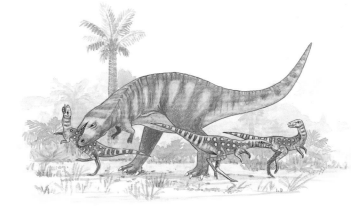

On the edge of the Great Sandy Desert is the Wolfe Creek meteorite crater, the second largest crater in the world from which fragments of a meteorite have been collected. The Aboriginal people, who called it *Kandimalal*, believe that the nearby Sturt and Wolfe Creeks show where two rainbow snakes crossed the desert. The crater is the place where one snake emerged from the ground. It was discovered by Europeans in 1947, during an aerial survey. This striking feature is protected by a national park.

DESCRIPTION: The crater is 900 metres across and almost perfectly circular. The floor is about 60 metres below the rim, and is flat but rises slightly in the centre. The porous gypsum found here supports reasonably large trees and contains a number of sinkholes that may reflect the position of stress fractures formed by the impact from the meteorite.

ROCK TYPES: The area in which the crater has formed is quartzite capped with laterite. The quartzite is clearly visible on the inner walls. The laterite which once capped the quartzite can now be seen in some places sandwiched between layers of quartzite, deformed by the force of the meteorite's impact.

LANDFORM FORMATION: The crater was formed by an enormous explosion when a meteorite weighing thousands of tonnes plunged to Earth around 300,000 years ago. It may have been up to 200 metres deep before it was filled by windblown sand and gypsum.

NOTABLE FEATURES: You may be able to locate rusty balls of rock, known as "shale-balls" on the top of the slopes of the crater, particularly on the western side. Some of these are scattered on the ground, but other chunks are fused into the laterite capping. They contain iron-nickel and iron-phosphide and are believed to be the deeply rusted remains of iron meteorites. Similar rocks are associated with other large craters around the world.

Photo - WA Tourism Commission

Photo - Ian Oswald-Jacobs

NOTE: The remnants of other meteorite craters have been recognised elsewhere in the Kimberley. These include Goat Paddock, north of Louisa Downs, the Spider near Mount Barnett Station on the Gibb River Road, and the Piccaninny Structure on top of the Bungle Bungle Range, in Purnululu National Park.

The presence of iron ore has been known from the islands of Yampi Sound since the early pearling fleets used it as ballast while operating along the Kimberley coastline. The ore, known as hematite, is high grade (up to 69 per cent iron). Two large iron ore mines were established in the area after the Second World War, firstly at Cockatoo Island (now abandoned) in 1951, and then at Koolan Island, which is still operating.

DESCRIPTION: Heading north from King Sound, the coastline is a succession of coral reefs, rugged islands, sea cliffs up to 150 metres high, and headlands separating inlets and bays, where tidal mudflats are fringed by mangroves. Sandy beaches are rare, occurring in sheltered bays.

ROCK TYPES: The rocks forming the coastline consist mainly of sandstones that were deposited in the Kimberley Basin between 1835 and 1790 million years ago (see page 14).

LANDFORM FORMATION: The present coastline has been produced by the drowning of the previously uplifted and eroded Kimberley surfaces. The system of hills and river valleys were flooded due to the worldwide rise in sea levels, following the end of the last ice age 17,000 years ago.

NOTABLE FEATURES: In the Buccaneer Archipelago, the rocks have been buckled into large folds, and broken along fault lines by major earth movements about 1000 million years ago and 560 million years ago. At the Horizontal Falls the folding has resulted in the rocks being tilted so that they are nearly vertical. The sea has breached a sandstone unit through a narrow gap, probably eroding its way along a crack or joint, and has hollowed out a wider inlet in the softer mudstones and shales behind. Massive tides (up to 11 metres) affect the coastline and at high tide the inlet is filled by the sea, but when the tide turns the water has to drain out through the narrow gap. The tide falls faster than the

Above: *Horizontal waterfall*   Below: *Folding, Buccaneer Archipelago*

water can escape, producing a "horizontal" waterfall. By low tide the inlet has emptied, but with the turn of the tide it fills again, resulting in a waterfall in the reverse direction.

Further north, the sandstones are generally flat lying. The sea formed St George Basin by eroding along a joint through the sandstone and into less resistant basaltic volcanic rocks. The joint continues through sandstones to the south-west, where it has controlled the course of the Prince Regent River.

Two major river systems dominate the drainage of the Kimberley region. The Fitzroy River enters the sea at King Sound near Derby, and the Ord River flows into Cambridge Gulf near Wyndham. Both river systems have wide floodplains, and their mouths are a complex system of tidal channels, mangrove swamps, and mud and samphire flats.

DESCRIPTION: Narrow tidal channels form complex, branching patterns in the mudflats. Mangrove swamps fringe major channels along the lower margins of the extensive bare, salty mudflats. Large proportions of these mudflats are only inundated by the sea during the higher tides. Above the mudflats, just above the high tide mark, there are extensive areas of densely vegetated samphire flats and low sand dunes, covered mainly by low saltbush, which grade into river floodplains vegetated with grasslands and woodlands.

LANDFORM FORMATION: Present day deposition of sediment is taking place on the river mouths and floodplains. The rivers only flow after prolonged and heavy rains, usually associated with tropical cyclones which hit the area every few years. Extensive flooding dumps large volumes of sediment into the sea and onto the wide floodplains. The channels, mudflats and mangrove swamps around the rivers' mouths also reflect the influence of the large tidal ranges (up to 11 metres) that affect the Kimberley coastline.

NOTABLE FEATURES: The river mouths and floodplains are made up of muds, silts and sands, eroded from across the Kimberley. The mudflats are an example of sedimentary rock formation in action. Over the next few thousands to millions of years, these sediments, together with the remains of plants and animals living on or within them, will be buried by more sediment. The weight of overlying sediment, and the action of

Photo – Courtesy of the WA Tourism Commission

fluids, rich in silica or calcium carbonate, flowing through them will cement the mud particles and sand grains together, turning the unconsolidated sediment into solid rock.

ROWLEY SHOALS

The coral atolls of the Rowley Shoals are renowned for their almost untouched coral gardens, giant clams and other shellfish and large and plentiful reef fish. The Shoals rise with nearly vertical sides from very deep water. About 300 kilometres offshore from Broome, they offer some of the best diving in Australia. They are regarded as the most perfect examples of shelf atolls in Australian waters.

DESCRIPTION: The Rowley Shoals are a chain of coral atolls along the edge of one of the widest continental shelves in the world. The three atolls have shallow lagoons inhabited by corals and abundant marine life. Each atoll covers an area of around 80 to 90 square kilometres. The three shoals are strikingly similar in dimension, shape, orientation and distance apart. Each atoll is north-south orientated, and slightly pear-shaped, with the narrow end towards the north. Mermaid Reef, the most northerly, rises from depths of about 440 metres, Clerke from 390 metres and Imperieuse from about 230 metres.

LANDFORM FORMATION: The Rowley Shoals lie on the very edge of Australia's continental shelf. Around 15 million years ago the shelf probably formed the shore of the mainland, which was fringed by a reef. The three shoals were possibly once reefs surrounding former headlands. As a result of changes in sea level and other geological processes (probably related to the northward drift of Australia towards Asia), these subsided into the sea, slowly enough for the fringing coral reefs to be maintained. As a result, the three reefs built up from the sea floor like high turrets, each enclosing a shallow lagoon. The growth of similar reefs along the shelf was not sufficient to keep pace with subsistence and there are a number of drowned reefs along the shelf, including one south of Imperieuse Reef. Further north, similar processes have formed the Scott and Seringpatam Reefs.

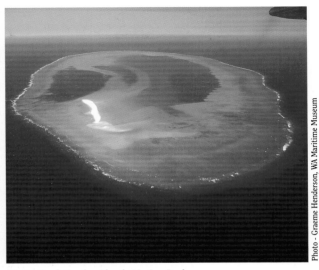

Clerke Reef, Rowley Shoals Marine Park

NOTABLE FEATURES: The Shoals have an unusually high tidal range for oceanic islands. When the tide is low, their reef flats stand like dam walls enclosing huge lakes, several metres above the surrounding sea. Water gushes from the narrow channels in the atolls in powerful torrents, like fast-flowing rivers. At high tide, the reefs disappear beneath the sea, with only the sandy islands of Clerke and Imperieuse Reefs visible.

VISITING RECORD

LANDFORM	NOTES
Kimberley Plateau	
Mitchell Plateau	
Bow River to Duffer Range	
McIntosh Hills	
Glacial Deposits	
Carr Boyd Ranges	
Argyle Diamond Mine	
Osmond Range	
Bungle Bungle Range	
Hidden Valley	
Ord Plains	
Halls Creek Fault	
China Wall, Halls Creek	

Photo - Carolyn Thomson

Tunnel Creek National Park

VISITING RECORD

LANDFORM	NOTES
Wolfe Creek Crater	
Gibb River Road granites	
King Leopold Ranges	
Durack Range	
Bell Creek Gorge	
Geikie Gorge	
Windjana Gorge	
Tunnel Creek	
Mimbi Caves	
Dinosaur footprints	
Buccaneer Archipelago	
Coastal mudflats	
Rowley Shoals	

Photo - WA Tourism Commission

Sandstones at Gantheaume Point, Broome

INDEX

Argyle Diamond Mine 5, 32-33, 58

Bell Creek Gorge 38-39

Broome sandstone 60-61

Buccaneer Archipelago 64-65

Bungle Bungle Range 50-55

Carlton Gorge 30-31

Carr Boyd Ranges 30-31

Cockatoo Island 64-65

China Wall 18-19, 56

Devonian barrier reef 42-49

Devonian sandstones 50-55

diamonds 5, 32-33, 58

dinosaur footprints 60-61

Durack Range 26-27

Gantheaume Point 60-61, 71

Geikie Gorge 42-47

Gibb River Road granites 22-23

glacial deposits 34-37

Gogo fish 46

gold 18-19

Halls Creek gold country 18-19

Halls Creek Fault 56-58

Hidden Valley 50-54

horizontal waterfall 64-65

igneous rocks 12

Inglis Gap 26

Kimberley Plateau 14-15

King Leopold Ranges 26-27

Koolan Island 64-65

laterite 7

lava flows 40-41

McIntosh Hills 24-25

metamorphic rocks 13

meteorite craters 62-63

Mimbi Caves 48-49

Mitchell Plateau 7, 16-17

mudflats 66-67

Ord Plains 40-41

Osmand Range 28-29

Purnululu National Park 50-55

Ragged Range 50-54

Rowley Shoals 68-69

Ruby Queen gold mine 18-19

sedimentary rocks 13

Tickalara Metamorphics 20-21

Tunnel Creek 48-49

Windjana Gorge 42-47

Wolfe Creek Crater 62-63